W9-AUD-251

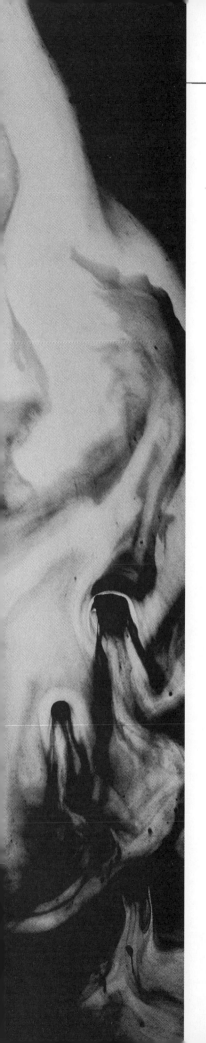

Bring Science Alive!®
Matter

TCi™

Chief Executive Officer
Bert Bower

Chief Operating Officer
Amy Larson

Strategic Process Director
Ellen Hardy

Director of Product Development
Maria Favata

Strategic Product Manager
Nathan Wellborne

Managing Editor
Ariel Stein

Senior Science Editor
Rebecca Ou

Senior Strategic Editor
Kim Merlino

***Space* Lead Editor**
Rebecca Ou

Science Content Developers
Karin Akre
Brennan Brockbank
Tanya Dewey
Mantissa Johnston
Douglas Le
Suzanne Lyons
Rebecca Ou
Ariel Stein
Clay Walton
Joan Westley
Jennifer Yeh

Editors
Helene Engler
Jill Farinelli
Mikaila Garfinkel
Sally Isaacs
Lauren Kent
Marlene Martzke
Tylar Pendgraft
Alex White

Writers
Sarah Martin
Linda Blumenthal
Sabre Duren
Katie Ewing
Rebecca Mikulec
Laura Prescott
Molly Wetterschneider

Illustrator/Graphic Artists
Andrew Dakhil
Martha Iserman
Aki Ruiz

Production and Design
Jodi Forrest
Jen Valenzuela
Michelle Vella

Web and Print Designer
Sarah Osentowski

Video Developer
Dominic Mercurio

Director of Operations
Marsha Ifurung

Investigation UX Testing
Davin Kunovsky

Software
Morris Thai
Robert Julius
Gabriel Redig

Software Quality Assurance
Mrudula Sarode

Art Direction
Julia Foug

TCi™

Teachers' Curriculum Institute
PO Box 1327
Rancho Cordova, CA 95741

Customer Service: 800-497-6138
www.teachtci.com

ISBN 978-1-58371-083-8

2 3 4 5 6 7 8 9 10 11 -DB- 23 22 21 20 19 18

Manufactured by Hess Print Solutions, Brimfield, OH
United States of America, July 2018, Job 272539

iii

Paul Ruscher, Ph.D.
Dean, Science Division
Lane Community College
Eugene, Oregon
Fellow, American Meteorological Society

Science Teacher Consultants

Kenneth Amunrud
Science Teacher
Joseph George Middle School
Alum Rock Union Elementary School District
San José, California

Nancy Anderson
Middle School Science Teacher
Mannington Township School
Mannington Township, New Jersey

Amy Argento
Science Teacher
Jefferson Middle School
Torrance Unified School District
Torrance, California

Noel Berghout
Math and Science Teacher
Jane Lathrop Stanford Middle School
Palo Alto Unified School District
Palo Alto, California

Carla Dalfonso
Science Specialist
Joe Serna Jr. Charter School
Lodi Unified School District
Lodi, California

Nora Haddad
Science Teacher
San Martin/Gwinn Environmental Science
Academy Morgan Hill Unified School District
Santa Clara County, California

Marsenne Kendall
Chemistry Teacher
Half Moon Bay High School
Cabrillo Unified School District
Half Moon Bay, California

Ann M. Lorey
Science Department Supervisor
and Instructional Coach
Jane Lathrop Stanford Middle School
Palo Alto Unified School District
Palo Alto, California

Kevin Lynch
Science Teacher
J.L. Stanford Middle School
Palo Alto Unified School District
Palo Alto, California

Michael Passow
Earth Science Teacher (ret.)
White Plains Middle School
White Plains, New York

Stephanie Ruzicka
Science Teacher
Horner Junior High School
Fremont Unified School District
Fremont, California

Michelle Serrano
Secondary Science Curriculum Specialist
Hemet Unified School District
Hemet, California

Mathematics Teacher Consultant

Kenneth Amunrud
Mathematics Teacher
Joseph George Middle School
Alum Rock Union Elementary
School District
San José, California

Reading Consultant

Marilyn Chambliss, Ph.D.
Associate Professor of Education Emerita
University of Maryland

CONTENTS

The Composition of Matter

States of Matter

Chemical Reactions

The Composition of Matter

Unit Overview

Phenomenon: To create stage makeup, chemists must account for the properties of the substances they will use.

Storyline: Analyze the properties of three different materials to identify the best material for a makeup pen to be used to transform actors into aliens. Then, write a pitch promoting the material you chose by describing its solubility, density, and suitability to use as alien makeup. Additionally, research the chemical formula and structure of a substance that makes up your material.

....

Atoms and Elements

Explore how everything is made of matter. Then, use your understanding of how the periodic table was developed to create your own periodic table of an object.

Molecules and Extended Structures

Use different tools to model simple molecules and more complex extended structures.

Substances and Their Properties

Learn about different properties that can be used to identify a substance. Then, perform experiments to identify an unknown substance from other ones that look similar but have different properties.

Performance Assessment: Determining the Best Material for a Makeup Pen Base

Read a letter from a client to identify the best material to work as the base for a makeup pen. After analyzing the properties of three different materials, identify the best material for your purposes. Then, use a model of a substance to determine its chemical formula and whether or not it is a molecule or extended structure. Finally, write and present a sales pitch explaining your results.

ANCHORING PHENOMENON

Anchoring Phenomenon: To create stage makeup, chemists must account for the properties of the substances they will use.

1. Complete the first two columns of this chart.

    • List what you think you already know about this unit's phenomenon.
    • Then write at least three questions you have about this phenomenon.

    Return to this chart at the end of the unit. Add the key information you learned about this phenomenon. Give evidence!

Know	Want to Know	Learned

Atoms and Elements

OBSERVING PHENOMENA

1. Record the mass of the balloons before and after you inflated them. Then, determine the mass of the air in each balloon.

Balloon	Mass of Balloon Before (g)	# of Breaths	Mass of Balloon After (g)	Mass of Air in Balloon (g)
A		2		
B		3		
C		4		
D		5		

Phenomenon: Balloons weigh more when filled with more air, despite air being invisible to the eye.

2. What questions do you have about this phenomenon?

INVESTIGATION 1

1. Sort the objects that you saw in your classroom by whether or not they are made of matter.

Matter	Non-Matter

2. List the objects in the video that can be classified as matter or non-matter.

Matter	Non-Matter

3. Describe the difference between matter and energy to your partner.

....

4 Atoms and Elements

© Teachers' Curriculum Institute

1 - Atoms

1. Look carefully at the list of objects and number them from smallest to largest, with "1" being the smallest and "5" being the largest.

ant	
atom	
cell	
dust particle	
ping pong ball	

INVESTIGATION 2

1. Record how many times you could cut the foil in half.

2. Record the following numbers in standard form.

Scientific Notation	Standard Form
2.23×10^{22} atoms	
1.43×10^{-14} meters	

3. Record the following numbers in scientific form in your notebook.

Standard Form	Scientific Notation
11,100,000,000,000,000,000,000 cuts	
3,500,000,000,000 centuries	
3,500,000,000,000 centuries as years	

4. Record the size category you were given here.

5. Choose five objects and sort them by the size category you were given.

Objects	Predicted Order	Actual Order

1. Heinrich Rohrer and Gerd Binnig were trying to solve the problem of seeing atoms directly. List the criteria and constraints of the problem they were trying to solve.

Criteria	Constraints

2. Suppose you were an engineer trying to solve the problem of identifying the element of an atom. You need to build a tool to do so. What are your criteria? What constraints do you think you might have?

Criteria	Constraints

INVESTIGATION 3

1. Record your topic here.

2. Record the elements related to your topic here.

3. What important information will you include in your periodic table? Record your notes here.

4. Organize your lists into groups. Record the name of each group in the top row, and list all of the elements in the group below.

5. Create your periodic table below. Be sure to include a key so everyone can read your table.

3 - Classifying Elements

1. Copper, silver, and gold are three elements often grouped together. They are also often called coinage metals. Why do you think that is?

Copper

Cu 63.5

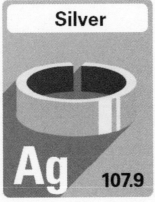

Silver

Ag 107.9

Gold

Au 197.0

1. Many scientists organized elements into tables. Compare Dmitry Mendeleev's periodic table to John Newland's periodic table. What similarities do you notice? What differences do you notice? Write a paragraph explaining your observations.

Dmitry Mendeleev's periodic table

Reihen	Gruppo I. — R²O	Gruppo II. — RO	Gruppo III. — R²O³	Gruppo IV. RH⁴ RO²	Gruppo V. RH³ R²O⁵	Gruppo VI. RH² RO³	Gruppo VII. RH R²O⁷	Gruppo VIII. — RO⁴
1	H=1							
2	Li=7	Be=9,4	B=11	C=12	N=14	O=16	F=19	
3	Na=23	Mg=24	Al=27,8	Si=28	P=31	S=32	Cl=35,5	
4	K=39	Ca=40	—=44	Ti=48	V=51	Cr=52	Mn=55	Fe=56, Co=59, Ni=59, Cu=63.
5	(Cu=63)	Zn=65	—=68	—=72	As=75	Se=78	Br=80	
6	Rb=85	Sr=87	?Yt=88	Zr=90	Nb=94	Mo=96	—=100	Ru=104, Rh=104, Pd=106, Ag=108.
7	(Ag=108)	Cd=112	In=113	Sn=118	Sb=122	Te=125	J=127	
8	Cs=133	Ba=137	?Di=138	?Ce=140	—	—	—	—
9	(—)	—	—	—	—	—	—	
10	—	—	?Er=178	?La=180	Ta=182	W=184	—	Os=195, Ir=197, Pt=198, Au=199.
11	(Au=199)	Hg=200	Tl=204	Pb=207	Bi=208	—	—	— — — —
12	—	—	—	Th=231	—	U=240	—	— — — —

John Newland's periodic table

No.		No.		No.		No.		No.		No.		No.		No.	
H	1	F	8	Cl	15	Co & Ni	22	Br	29	Pd	36	I	42	Pt & Ir	50
Li	2	Na	9	K	16	Cu	23	Rb	30	Ag	37	Cs	44	Os	51
G	3	Mg	10	Ca	17	Zn	24	Sr	31	Cd	38	Ba & V	45	Hg	52
Bo	4	Al	11	Cr	19	Y	25	Ce & La	33	U	40	Ta	46	Tl	53
C	5	Si	12	Ti	18	In	26	Zr	32	Sn	39	W	47	Pb	54
N	6	P	13	Mn	20	As	27	Di & Mo	34	Sb	41	Nb	48	Bi	55
O	7	S	14	Fe	21	Se	28	Ro & Ru	35	Te	43	Au	49	Th	56

© Teachers' Curriculum Institute

5 - Using the Periodic Table

Use the periodic table to answer the questions that follow.

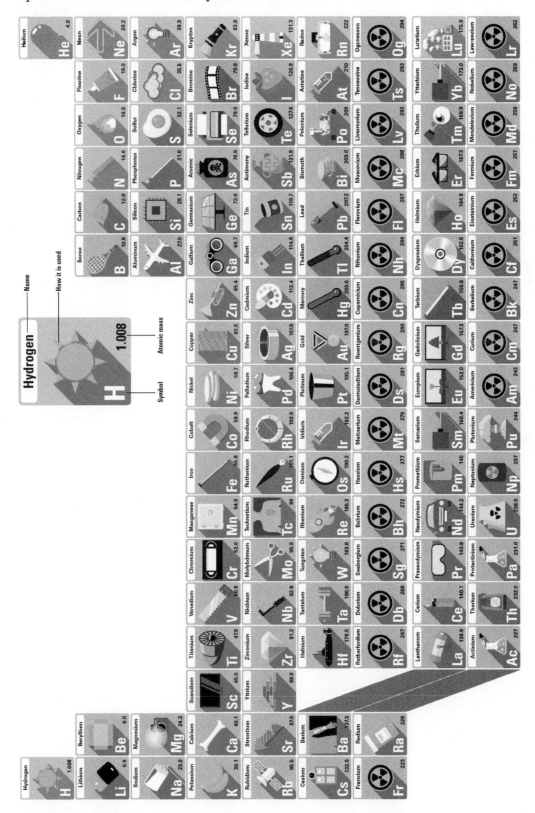

1. What are the names of the following elements?

    - Cu
    - Li
    - Ni
    - O
    - Pd
    - Po
    - Pt
    - S
    - Zn

2. Look closely at the location of each of these elements on the periodic table. Make a prediction: which elements have similar properties to each other and why?

MAKING SENSE OF PHENOMENA

Phenomenon: Balloons weigh more when filled with more air, despite air being invisible to the eye.

1. Use what you have learned to explain this phenomenon.

2. Record your notes from your internet research on one of the following categories of the periodic table:

   - Noble gases
   - Radioactive Elements
   - Transition Metals
   - Semi-metals
   - Non-Metals

3. Write a paragraph that describes what makes them similar to each other, and different form other groups of elements.

4. List the common uses of the category you researched.

Molecules and Extended Structures

OBSERVING PHENOMENA

1. List all of the materials you can see in each image.

List of all Materials	List of all Materials	List of all Materials	List of all Materials
Total Materials	Total Materials	Total Materials	Total Materials
Similarities	Similarities	Similarities	Similarities
Differences	Differences	Differences	Differences

Phenomenon: The millions and millions of types of materials in the world are composed of some combination of only 92 different types of atoms.

2. What questions do you have about this phenomenon?

INVESTIGATION 1

1. Record the color and number of bonds possible for each atom type.

Atom Type	Model Color	Bonds Possible
Hydrogen		
Oxygen		
Nitrogen		
Carbon		

2. Fill out the table for simple molecules.

Substance Name	Model	Chemical Formula	Number of Elements	Number of Atoms	Number of Bonds
Hydrogen gas		H_2			
Oxygen gas		O_2			
Nitrogen gas		N_2			
Nitrogen Monoxide		NO			

3. Fill out the table for other simple molecules.

Substance Name	Model	Chemical Formula	Number of Elements	Number of Atoms	Number of Bonds
Ammonia		NH_3			
Water		H_2O			
Hydrogen Peroxide		H_2O_2			
Carbon Dioxide		CO_2			

4. Fill out the table for complex molecules.

Substance Name	Model	Chemical Formula	Number of Elements	Number of Atoms	Number of Bonds
Methane		CH_4			
Ethane		C_2H_6			
Propane		C_3H_8			
Propene		C_3H_6			
Propyne		C_3H_4			

5. Describe the model of polyester you created. Explain how your model is a good model for polyester. Then, describe any problems with your model.

6. Describe the model of salt that you created. Explain how your model is a good model for salt. Then, describe any problems with your model.

7. Describe the model of ice that you created. Explain how your model is a good model for ice. Then, describe any problems with your model.

1. Look closely at this model. Circle all of the chemical bonds in red. Then, circle all of the atoms in blue.

2. Explain why the above model is a good representation of a molecule. Be sure to include the following terms in your answer: *atom* and *chemical bond*.

3. Different models have benefits and drawbacks. What is a drawback of the above model? Explain how you would improve the above model.

2 - Composition and Structure of Molecules

Look closely at this molecule to answer the following question.

1. Identify the atomic composition of the molecule. Then, describe its chemical structure.

Atomic Composition	Chemical Structure

3 - Crystals and Polymers

1. Describe the difference between a molecule and an extended structure.

2. Fill out the blanks in the table for the following crystals.

Crystal	Ratio	Atom 1		Atom 2	
Table salt (NaCl)	1:1	Sodium atoms:	275	Chlorine atoms:	
Quartz (SiO_2)	1:2	Silicon atoms:		Oxygen atoms:	560
Iron rust (Fe_2O_3)	2:3	Iron atoms:		Oxygen atoms:	744
Lead iodide (PbI_2)		Lead atoms:	252	Iodine atoms:	504

3. Crystals and polymers are different types of extended structures. Think of a crystal of molecules, such as ice. What are the similarities and differences between a crystal of molecules and a polymer?

Similarities	Differences

1. Look at this model of polyester and this model of salt. Describe what patterns you notice.

Polyester	Table Salt
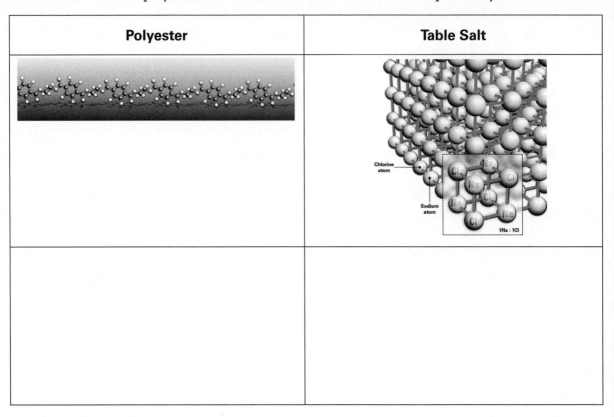	

2. How do you think the patterns in the atomic structure affect the patterns that you can see?

MAKING SENSE OF PHENOMENA

1. Write a paragraph explaining why diamond is one of the strongest materials on Earth, while graphite is used in pencils. Be sure to use the words *atom* and *extended structure*.

2. Write a paragraph explaining why coal may be used in makeups and dyes, but graphite and diamond cannot. Be sure to use the words *atom* and *extended structure*.

Phenomenon: The millions and millions of types of materials in the world are composed of some combination of only 92 different types of atoms.

3. Use what you have learned to explain this phenomenon.

Molecules and Extended Structures

OBSERVING PHENOMENA

1. What will happen if you shake the column?

2. Why do you think the liquids settled in the same order as they originally appeared?

Phenomenon: Some liquids do not mix with other liquids, so they form distinct layers when poured in a bottle.

3. What questions do you have about this phenomenon?

1 - Substances

1. Describe the difference between a molecule of water and the substance water.

2. Macroscopic means that it is at a scale you can see with your eyes. Explain why you cannot see a macroscopic amount of air.

Look closely at the gold jewelry shown below to answer the following questions.

1. List all of the properties that the jewelry has.

2. Sort the properties you listed into properties that are shared by all objects of that substance and properties that are not shared.

Shared Properties	Not Shared Properties

1. Predict what will happen when you place the regular soda in the water. What will happen when you place the diet soda in the water? Explain your reasoning.

2. Predict which objects will float in water and which will sink.

Object	Float/Sink

3. What do you think causes an object to float or to sink? Explain your reasoning.

30 Molecules and Extended Structures

© Teachers' Curriculum Institute

4. Record your data in the table below. Be sure to label all of your columns.

Object	Mass	Float/Sink		

5. Revise your prediction to account for the other variable you have just learned about.

1. Density is the amount of mass per unit volume. Look around you. What is the most dense object that you can see? Why is it the most dense?

2. Calculate the density of the following objects.

Object	Mass (g)	Volume (mL)	Density (g/mL)
Oxygen	1.4	1000	
Water	150	150	
Hydrogen peroxide	174	120	
Iron	787	100	
Iron Oxide	262	50	

3. List the objects in order from least dense to most dense.

4. Does any result surprise you? Explain your reasoning.

INVESTIGATION 2

1. Record your observations on the solubility of different substances in water.

Substance	Solubility in water (y/n)
Hydrogen peroxide	
Isopropyl alcohol	
Mineral oil	
Vinegar	

2. Record your observations on the solubility of inks in various liquids.

	Water	Hydrogen peroxide	Isopropyl alcohol	Mineral oil	Vinegar
Permanent Marker					
Wet Erase Marker					
Ink Pen					

3. List out your plan for your investigation.

Amount of solid to be used	
Amount of liquid to be used	

4. Record all of your observations from your investigation here.

    •   In the first row, list all of the liquids you will test.
    •   In the first column, list all of the solids you will test.
    •   Then, record whether or not the solids are soluble or not.

4 - Melting and Boiling Point

1. What is happening in this image? What do you expect to happen?

2. Explain why you can boil water in a pot without the pot also boiling.

5 - Solubility

1. This is an image of sugar being poured into a bowl of water. Based on what you see in this image, what do you expect to happen?

2. What do you expect to see if you poured sand into water?

1. Record the density results from the laboratory here. Then, for each unknown, list what substances they could possibly be.

	Density	Substance?
Substance on floor		
Substance on shoe		

2. Record the solubility results from the laboratory here. Then, for each unknown, list what substances they could possibly be.

	Solubility in water	Solubility in oil	Substance?
Unknown on floor			
Unknown on shoe			

3. Record the flammability results from the laboratory here. Then, for each unknown, list what substances they could possibly be.

	Flammability Result	Substance?
Unknown on floor		
Unknown on shoe		

4. Record the boiling point results from the laboratory here. Then, for each unknown, list what substances they could possibly be.

	Boiling Point Result	Substance?
Unknown on floor		
Unknown on shoe		

5. Organize your data in one table. Then, list what you think each unknown substance is.

	Density	Solubility in water	Solubility in oil	Flammability	Boiling Point	Substance?
Unknown on floor						
Unknown on shoe						

6. Using your data, explain your reasoning for what each unknown substance is.

1. What is happening in this image? What do you expect to happen?

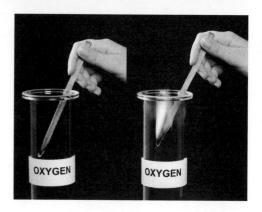

A scientist was trying to identify two unknown substances. Look closely at the table of results for their data.

Substance	Density (g/cm³)	Melting Point (°C)	Solubility in Water	Flammability
acetominophen	1.263	169	no	yes
asprin	1.4	135	yes	yes
cellulose	1.5	500	no	yes
ibuprofen	1.03	75	no	yes
naproxen	1.2	152	no	yes

2. Compare the above table of known substances to the data below to identify the unknown substances.

Table of Results					
Unknown	Density	Melting Point	Solubility in Water	Flammability	Substance
Unknown A	1.3	150	yes	yes	
Unknown B	1.4	148	no	yes	

7 - Mixtures

1. Look around your classroom. Choose two macroscopic objects or materials and research them to identify if they are substances or mixtures. If the object or material is a mixture, list two substances that make up the object or material.

Object or Material	Substance or Mixture?	Names of 2 Substances

MAKING SENSE OF PHENOMENA

Phenomenon: The millions and millions of types of materials in the world are composed of some combination of only 92 different types of atoms.

1. Use what you have learned to explain this phenomenon.

2. Suppose you were developing a permanent marker. A marker is made of the following components:

   - Pigment that stays on the paper.
   - Base that moves the pigment.

   Write a letter to your friend explaining what properties would be important for your pigment and what properties would be important for your base. Be sure to explain your reasoning. Your letter should include the terms: *density, solubility, boiling point,* and *flammability.*

Determining the Best Material for a Makeup Pen Base

Throughout this unit, you have been learning about the characteristics of matter. You learned about the smallest particles of matter, atoms, and how the different elements are organized on the periodic table. You modeled how atoms combined into molecules and extended structures. You then collected data on different properties to identify substances.

Now it's time to show what you know by analyzing three materials and writing a pitch promoting one material for a makeup pen base.

At Theater Cosmetics Inc., you have been asked to develop a new makeup pen base for a show about aliens. You will analyze three different materials to determine the best one for your client. You will research one of the substances in this material to describe its atomic composition and structure. To promote the best product, you will have to point to the specific properties this material has!

Performance Assessment Requirements
Your pitch should demonstrate knowledge of:
- how to identify the chemical formula of a substance from a model.
- whether or not the substance is a molecule or extended structure.
- how to measure the solubility and density of a material.
- how to evaluate the properties of a material to determine its suitability for a specific task.

_____ Step 1: Identifying Properties

List the properties of the base that your makeup pen should have.

_____ **Step 2: Evaluating Properties**

Measure the density of the three materials. Record your results here.

Oil Base	Volume (ml)	Mass (g)	Density = mass / volume (g/ml)
Mineral Oil			
Olive Oil			
Petroleum Jelly			

Measure the solubility of the three materials in salt water. Record your results here.

Oil Base	Solubility in Salt Water
Mineral Oil	
Olive Oil	
Petroleum Oil	

Record the melting points of the three materials here.

Oil Base	Melting Point
Mineral Oil	
Olive Oil	
Petroleum Oil	

_____ **Step 3: Determining a Makeup Pen Base**

Which material do you recommend for use in the makeup pen base? Explain why.

Explain how the chemical formula of a substance models that substance. What does it show? What does it leave out?

What is the chemical formula of the substance on your handout?

Is this substance a molecule or extended structure? Explain your reasoning.

_____ **Step 4: Writing a Pitch**

Write your sales pitch for the base you are recommending. Your pitch should include the following:

- The chemical formula of one of the substances in the material you are recommending.
- Whether or not the substance is a molecule or an extended structure, and why.
- A description of its properties, such as its: density, melting/boiling point, solubility in salt water, flammability, and odor.
- An explanation of why its properties make it a good base for your client's new makeup pen.

_____ **Step 5: Presenting your Pitch**

Take notes on your classmates' pitches here.

Performance Assessment Rubric

Use the rubric to evaluate your work on this Performance Assessment.

Dimension	Achievement Levels			Score
	Proficient (2 points)	Emergent (1 point)	Not Present (0 points)	
Science and Engineering Practices Developing and Using Models *Develop a model to predict and/or describe phenomena.*	Used a model to determine the chemical formula of a substance and whether or not it is a molecule or extended structure.	Used a model to determine the chemical formula of a substance but did not determine whether or not it is a molecule or extended structure.	Did not determine the chemical formula of a substance.	
Analyzing and Interpreting Data *Analyze and interpret data to determine similarities and differences in findings.*	Analyzed and interpreted data on the three mixtures to determine which one best fit a client's needs.	Analyzed and interpreted data on the three mixtures but did not explain why it best fit a client's needs.	Did not analyze and interpret data.	
Crosscutting Concepts Scale, Proportion and Quantity *Time, space, and energy phenomena can be observed at various scales using models to study systems that are too large or too small.*	Used a model to identify the chemical formula of a substance too small to be seen.	Used a model to identify the chemical formula of a substance too small to be seen.	Did not identify the chemical formula of a substance too small to be seen.	
Disciplinary Core Ideas Structure and Properties of Matter *Substances are made from different types of atoms, which combine with one another in various ways. Atoms form molecules that range in size from two to thousands of atoms.* *Solids may be formed from molecules, or they may be extended structures with repeating subunits (e.g., crystals).*	Described the atomic composition of a substance.	Incorrectly described the atomic composition of a substance.	Did not describe the chemical formula of a substance.	
	Determined and explained whether or not a substance is a molecule or extended structures.	Determined if a substance is a molecule or extended structure, but did not explain why.	Did not determine if a substance is a molecule or extended structure.	
Each pure substance has characteristic physical and chemical properties (for any bulk quantity under given conditions) that can be used to identify it.	Identified characteristic physical and chemical properties of a substance to determine its suitability as a pen base.	Identified characteristic physical and chemical properties of a substance but did not determine its suitability as a pen base.	Did not identify the properties of a substance.	

States of Matter

Unit Overview

Phenomenon: Ice eventually turns into water when it is left out, and water boils and seems to disappear when it is heated.

Storyline: The particle motion of atoms and molecules results in the three common states of matter that can be observed—solid, liquid, and gas. Write a letter to an alien visiting Earth that explains how a molecule of water on Earth changes state and compares with state changes on the alien's planet.

The Motion of Particles

Develop a model that shows the relationship between particle motion and states of matter. Then, learn about the effect of pressure and temperature on particle motion and predict state changes as a result of pressure and temperature changes.

Heat, Temperature, and State Changes

Deepen your understanding of how state changes occur by first comparing the difference between heat, temperature, and thermal energy. Then, explore six different types of state changes with videos and hands-on experiments to apply your understanding of how thermal energy affects state changes.

Performance Assessment: Writing to your Alien Pen Pal

Share your understanding of states of matter by writing back to your alien pen pal explaining the natural phenomena of states of matter.

ANCHORING PHENOMENON

Anchoring Phenomenon: Ice eventually turns into water when it is left out, and water boils and seems to disappear when it is heated.

1. Complete the first two columns of this chart.

   • List what you think you already know about this unit's phenomenon.
   • Then write at least three questions you have about this phenomenon.

   Return to this chart at the end of the unit. Add the key information you learned about this phenomenon. Give evidence!

Know	Want to Know	Learned

The Motion of Particles

1. How would you describe the motion of the blue and yellow dyes once they were added to the beaker?

2. How might you explain why the dye molecules did not go straight to the bottom of the beaker or move in straight lines?

3. Which sample of water required the most time to completely turn green?

4. What might the green color signify?

5. How was the macroscopic behavior of the dye in Beaker A different from Beaker B and Beaker C?

6. Use your understanding of particles and substances to construct an explanation for what you observed during this activity.

Phenomenon: Drops of food coloring dissolve into water at very different rates depending on the temperature of the water.

7. What questions do you have about this phenomenon?

Using the simulation, investigate states of matter. Then, answer the following questions.

1. Change the state of matter to Solid by choosing the tab on the right. How would you describe the molecular motion?

2. Change the state of matter to Liquid by choosing the tab on the right. How would you describe the molecular motion?

3. Change the state of matter to Gas by choosing the tab on the right. How would you describe the molecular motion?

4. Compare the computer model in the simulation to the model of states of matter you performed in class using your bodies. What are the advantages and disadvantages of each?

1 - Molecular Motion in Solids

1. Draw the particle motion of a solid.

2. How does the particle motion of a solid affect its macroscopic behavior?

2 - Molecular Motion in Liquids

1. Draw the particle motion of a liquid.

2. How does the particle motion of a liquid affect its macroscopic behavior?

1. Draw the particle motion of a gas.

2. How does the particle motion of a gas affect its macroscopic behavior?

3. How does the particle motion and behavior affect how a substance appears on a macroscopic level? Use the terms *solid*, *liquid*, *gas*, *state of matter*, and *particle motion* in your answer.

INVESTIGATION 2

1. How would you describe the molecules in the high pressure column at the beginning of the activity?

2. After the pressure changed in the high pressure column, what state did the molecules most closely represent at the end of the activity?

3. How would you describe the molecules in the low pressure column at the beginning of the activity?

4. After the pressure changed in the low pressure column, what state did the molecules most closely represent at the end of the activity?

1. Draw the particle motion of these substances at the following temperatures.

2. Using what you know of particle motion in solids, liquids, and gases, explain why you think temperature changes affect a substance's state of matter. Use the terms *particle motion*, *temperature*, *solid*, *liquid*, and *gas* in your answer.

1. Use arrows to indicate the pressure the gas particles exert on the inside and outside of the containers.

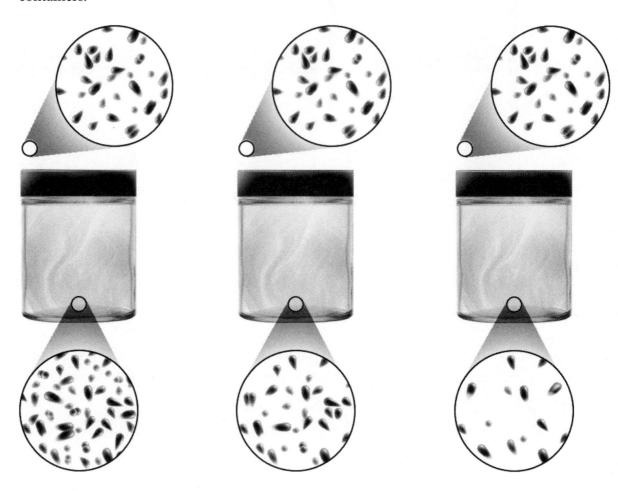

2. Draw the particle motion of these substances at the following pressures.

3. Using what you know of particle motion in solids, liquids, and gases, explain why you think pressure changes affect a substance's state of matter. Use the terms *particle motion*, *pressure*, *solid*, *liquid*, and *gas* in your answer.

1. Look closely at this state diagram.

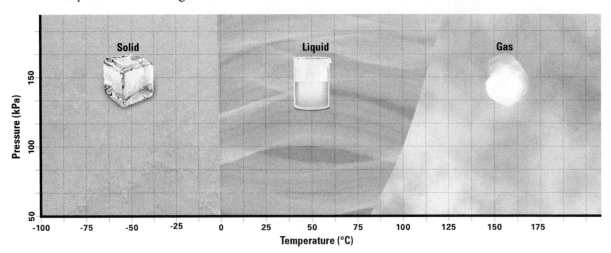

Use the state diagram to record the state of matter you would expect water to be in at each pressure and temperature.

Pressure (kPa)	Temperature (degrees Celsius)	State of Matter
70	-15	
70	25	
70	110	
101	-15	
101	25	
101	145	
160	-15	
160	25	
160	110	

You receive a letter from a scientist. Carefully read the letter and then answer the questions that follow.

> Help! I'm trying to perform an experiment that will take a whole day but the air conditioning in my laboratory is broken. The temperature goes from very chilly in the morning to very hot in the afternoon. Additionally, my laboratory is located at a high altitude in the mountains. I won't be able to perform my experiment at STP (100 kPa and 0 degrees Celsius). Can you help me design a tool to keep my laboratory at STP?

1. Design and draw a tool to keep the scientist's laboratory at STP.

2. Explain how your tool will keep the scientist's laboratory at STP.

MAKING SENSE OF PHENOMENA

Phenomenon: Drops of food coloring dissolve into water at very different rates depending on the temperature of the water.

1. Use what you have learned to explain this phenomenon.

Heat, Temperature, and State Changes

OBSERVING PHENOMENA

1. Using what you know about temperature and pressure and how they affect the motion of particles, make a prediction on how the motion of particles is related to the thermal energy of a substance.

2. Make a prediction on how the motion of particles is related to the heat it gains or loses from other substances.

Phenomenon: In a warm room, water droplets form on a can of cold liquid.

3. What questions do you have about this phenomenon?

Heat, Temperature, and State Changes   **61**

INVESTIGATION 1

1. How would you describe the motions of the copper atoms before and after the hot water was poured?

2. Did the thermal energy of the copper tubing increase or decrease when hot water was added? Cite evidence to support your claim.

3. How would you describe the motions of the copper atoms before and after the ice water was poured?

4. Did the thermal energy of the copper tubing increase or decrease when cold water was added? Cite evidence to support your claim.

5. Thermal energy transferred from a warmer object to a cooler object is called heat.

   Using the definition above, explain the feelings you experienced in your hands.

6. Use arrows to represent the direction of heat flow in each of the three containers of water.

 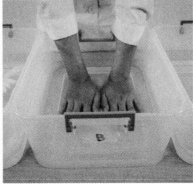 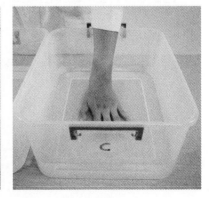

1. Circle the object with more thermal energy.

2. Explain your reasoning.

3. Circle the object with the higher temperature.

4. Explain your reasoning.

5. Draw arrows to describe the heat between each object and the air around them.

6. Explain your reasoning.

INVESTIGATION 2

1. Fill out the table as you watch each video.

	What do you observe in this video?	Is the substance gaining or losing thermal energy?	What state change do you see?
Video 1			
Video 2			
Video 3			
Video 4			
Video 5			
Video 6			

2. Annotate the diagram of **freezing**. Use the terms *heat, temperature, thermal energy, particles,* and *motion* to describe what happens on a microscopic and macroscopic level during **freezing**. Be sure to indicate the direction of heat flow.

3. Write your explanation of **freezing**.

4. Annotate the diagram of **melting**. Use the terms *heat, temperature, thermal energy, particles,* and *motion* to describe what happens on a microscopic and macroscopic level during **melting**. Be sure to indicate the direction of heat flow.

5. Write your explanation of **melting**.

6. Annotate the diagram of **condensing**. Use the terms *heat, temperature, thermal energy, particles,* and *motion* to describe what happens on a microscopic and macroscopic level during **condensing**. Be sure to indicate the direction of heat flow.

7. Write your explanation of **condensing**.

8. Annotate the diagram of **evaporating**. Use the terms *heat, temperature, thermal energy, particles,* and *motion* to describe what happens on a microscopic and macroscopic level during **evaporating**. Be sure to indicate the direction of heat flow.

9. Write your explanation of **evaporating**.

10. Annotate the diagram of **subliming**. Use the terms *heat, temperature, thermal energy, particles,* and *motion* to describe what happens on a microscopic and macroscopic level during **subliming**. Be sure to indicate the direction of heat flow.

11. Write your explanation of **subliming**.

12. Annotate the diagram of **depositing**. Use the terms *heat, temperature, thermal energy, particles,* and *motion* to describe what happens on a microscopic and macroscopic level during **depositing**. Be sure to indicate the direction of heat flow.

13. Write your explanation of **depositing**.

14. Use the terms *subliming*, *depositing*, *condensing*, *evaporating*, *melting*, and *freezing* to complete this diagram. For each transformation, indicate if heat is added or removed during the state change.

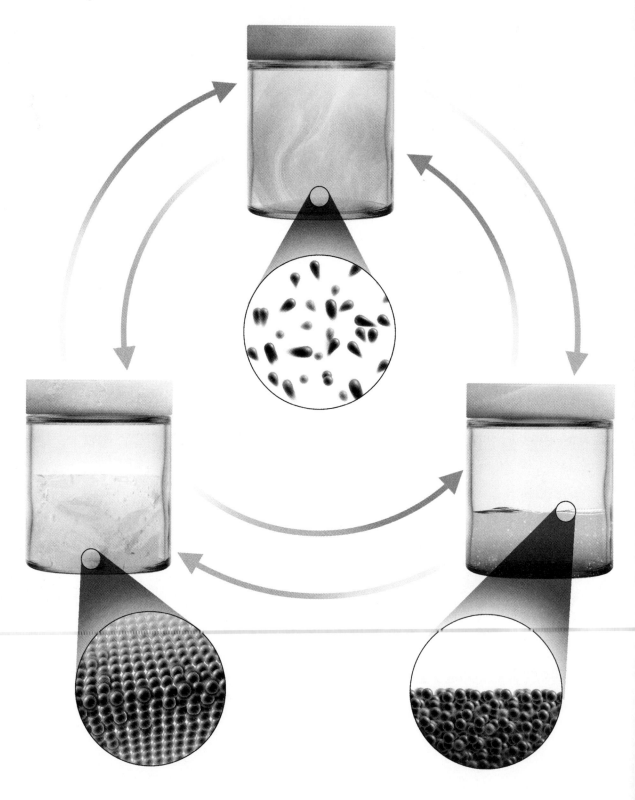

1. Draw and label the melting process.

2. Explain the melting process.

3. Draw and label the evaporating process.

4. Explain the evaporating process.

5. Draw and label the subliming process.

6. Explain the subliming process.

3 - Objects Lose Thermal Energy

1. Draw and label the condensing process.

2. Explain the condensing process.

3. Draw and label the freezing process.

Liquid   Solid

4. Explain the freezing process.

5. Draw and label the depositing process.

Gas   Solid

6. Explain the depositing process.

Use the data table to answer the following question.

	Melting Point (°C)	Boiling Point (°C)
Helium	-272.2	-268
Carbon Dioxide	-78.5 (sublimes)	
Water	0	100
Gallium	29.8	2403

1. Come up with a claim for which substance has the strongest attractions between its particles. Then, list the evidence and your reasoning.

Claim	
Evidence	
Reasoning	

MAKING SENSE OF PHENOMENA

Phenomenon: In a warm room, water droplets form on a can of cold liquid.

1. Use what you have learned to explain this phenomenon.

2. On a very hot day or during physical activity you have probably noticed moisture coming from the pores in your skin. Sweat is the body's natural method of regulating temperature. But why?

   Conduct an internet search to find out how sweat helps cool the body. Use the terms like *heat*, *thermal energy*, and *temperature*, to write a paragraph that demonstrates your understanding of energy movement during state changes by explaining how sweating helps keep humans cool when the temperature rises.

Writing to your Alien Pen Pal

Now you will show what you have learned about the practices, crosscutting concepts, and core ideas in this unit.

Your alien pen pal, Neila Lap, has been learning about your home planet as she prepares to visit.

Read her letter.

Your task will be to write a letter in reply that explains the states of matter using the motion of particles and how thermal energy affects the state of matter.

How can you explain this phenomenon to your alien pen pal, Neila Lap?

Performance Assessment Requirements

Your letter should demonstrate these ideas about states of matter:

*   the states of water on Earth, and where to find each one.
*   each state of water in terms of the motions of water molecules.
*   how thermal energy can affect the motion of water molecules.
*   the boiling and melting points of water on Earth and how they sometimes vary.
*   if Neila's planet is warmer or colder than where you live.
*   the type of clothing that you recommend she and her family bring for their visit.

_____ Step 1: Writing a Letter to Neila Lap

Write a letter to your Alien Pen Pal Neila Lap.

_____ **Step 2: Supporting Your Model Visually**

To support the conceptual model in your letter, include clearly labeled diagrams or illustrations below.

Performance Assessment Rubric

Use the rubric to evaluate your work on this Performance Assessment.

Dimension	Achievement Levels			Score
	Proficient (2 points)	**Emergent (1 point)**	**Not Present (0 points)**	
Science and Engineering Practices Develop and Use a Model *Develop a model to predict and/or describe phenomena.*	Developed a model to describe and predict the phenomena of state changes with changes in particle motion and thermal energy.	Developed a model to describe the phenomena of state changes with either changes in particle motion or thermal energy, but did not make predictions.	Did not develop a model to describe and predict the phenomena of state changes with changes in particle motion and thermal energy.	
Crosscutting Concepts Cause and Effect *Cause and effect relationships may be used to predict phenomena in natural or designed systems.*	Used the cause and effect relationships between particle motion and state of matter and between thermal energy and state of matter to predict state changes.	Used one of the cause and effect relationships between particle motion and state of matter or between thermal energy and state of matter to predict state changes.	Did not use cause and effect relationships to predict state changes.	
Disciplinary Core Ideas Structure and Properties of Matter *Gases and liquids are made of molecules or inert atoms that are moving about relative to each other. In a liquid, the molecules are constantly in contact with others; in a gas, they are widely spaced except when they happen to collide. In a solid, atoms are closely spaced and may vibrate in position but do not change relative locations. The changes of state that occur with variations in temperature or pressure can be described and predicted using these models of matter.*	Described how the particle motion of particles affect a substance's state of matter. In a solid, atoms are closely spaced and may vibrate in position but do not change relative locations. In a liquid, the molecules are constantly in contact with others. In a gas, they are widely spaced except when they happen to collide.	Described one or two of the following: In a solid, atoms are closely spaced and may vibrate in position but do not change relative locations. In a liquid, the molecules are constantly in contact with others. In a gas, they are widely spaced except when they happen to collide.	Did not describe how the particle motion of particles affect a substance's state of matter.	
	Described the changes of state that can occur with variations in temperature or pressure.	Described one or two of the following: how changes of state can occur with variations in temperature or pressure.	Did not describe the changes of state that can occur with variations in temperature or pressure.	

Dimension	Achievement Levels			Score
	Proficient (2 points)	Emergent (1 point)	Not Present (0 points)	
Disciplinary Core Ideas Definitions of Energy *The term "heat" as used in everyday language refers both to thermal energy (the motion of atoms or molecules within a substance) and the transfer of that thermal energy from one object to another. In science, heat is used only for this second meaning; it refers to the energy transferred due to the temperature difference between two objects. The temperature of a system is proportional to the average internal kinetic energy and potential energy per atom or molecule (whichever is the appropriate building block for the system's material). The details of that relationship depend on the type of atom or molecule and the interactions among the atoms in the material. Temperature is not a direct measure of a system's total thermal energy. The total thermal energy (sometimes called the total internal energy) of a system depends jointly on the temperature, the total number of atoms in the system, and the state of the material.*	Defined and explained heat as the energy transferred due to temperature differences between two objects.	Defined but did not explain heat as the energy transferred due to temperature differences between two objects.	Did not define or explain heat as the energy transferred due to temperature differences between two objects.	
	Defined and explained that thermal energy depends on the following: the temperature or average energy of the particles in the system; the total number of atoms in the system; and the state of the material.	Defined but did not explained that thermal energy depends on the following: the temperature or average energy of the particles in the system; the total number of atoms in the system; and the state of the material.	Did not define or explain that thermal energy depends on the following: the temperature or average energy of the particles in the system; the total number of atoms in the system; and the state of the material.	

Chemical Reactions

Unit Overview

Phenomenon: Survival kits often include portable gear, such as hot packs and butane torches, that can be activated at a moment's notice.

Storyline: The newest season of "The Next Top Survivalist" is looking for contestants, and you've been asked to audition! To prepare, you will explore how chemical reactions can help people survive when caught unaware in the wilderness.

Identifying Chemical Reactions

Test the properties of reactants and products to determine whether or not a chemical reaction has occurred.

Atoms in Chemical Reactions

Model the atoms before and after a chemical reaction to observe the changes to substances.

Energy in Chemical Reactions

Investigate exothermic and endothermic reactions that can be used for a chemical hand warmer or a cold pack.

Engineering Challenge: Designing a Hot Pack

Students design, build, and optimize a hot pack that meets agreed upon criteria and constraints.

Chemical Engineering and Society

Research and investigate different substances that have had profound impacts on society.

Performance Assessment: Modifying and Explaining Survival Gear

Create a short video-clip that demonstrates the supplies necessary to make a survival pack for the reality TV show, "The Next Top Survivalist."

ANCHORING PHENOMENON

Anchoring Phenomenon: Survival kits often include portable gear, such as hot packs and butane torches, that can be activated at a moment's notice.

1. Complete the first two columns of this chart.

   - List what you think you already know about this unit's phenomenon.
   - Then write at least three questions you have about this phenomenon.

   Return to this chart at the end of the unit. Add the key information you learned about this phenomenon. Give evidence!

Know	Want to Know	Learned

Identifying Chemical Reactions

Phenomenon: Mixing vinegar and baking soda causes the substances to bubble up and spill over a container's edge.

1. What questions do you have about this phenomenon?

INVESTIGATION 1

1. How do you think we can know when a new substance is formed from two original substances interacting? Write out your ideas.

2. Table 1: In the first column, write the list of properties you brainstormed. Then fill in the properties you observe before the substances undergo an interaction.

Property	Sugar	Steel Wool	Zinc	HCl

3. Table 2: Fill in the properties of the substances present after the original materials interact.

Property	Burned Sugar Product	Burned Steel Wool Product	Zinc and HCl Product

Burning Sugar

4. With what substance do you think the sugar is reacting?

5. Why don't these substances react when there is no fire?

6. Did a chemical reaction occur? Explain your answer.

Burning Steel Wool

7. With what substance do you think the steel wool is reacting?

8. Why don't these substances react when there is no fire?

9. Did a chemical reaction occur? Explain your answer.

Mixing Zinc and HCl

10. Why don't these substances react until they are mixed?

11. Did a chemical reaction occur? Explain your answer.

Review the list of properties that you made before observing the chemical reactions.

12. Did every property change in every reaction? Use an example to explain your answer.

13. Would you add any properties to the list now?

14. What general conclusion can you make about how chemical reactions change properties?

1. What is a chemical reaction?

2. Why isn't a state change from liquid to solid a chemical reaction?

3. When lead nitrate and potassium iodide are mixed, lead iodide and potassium nitrate form. What are the reactants and products in this chemical reaction?

Potassium
iodide

Lead
iodide

Lead
nitrate

4. What is the difference between chemical properties and physical properties?

1. Why don't matches catch on fire while they are in the box?

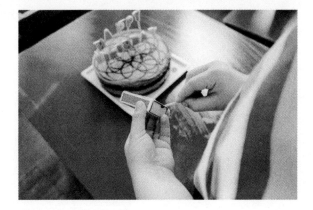

2. What are three conditions that can cause chemical reactions to occur?

3. Give an example of a chemical reaction that is caused when reactants cool.

4. Give an example of a chemical reaction that is caused when reactants are mixed.

INVESTIGATION 2

1. Can you tell by looking at the five white powders whether they are the same or different? Explain.

2. Table 1: Fill in the density and solubility of each substance as you measure it.

Substance	Density (g/cm³)	Soluble in Water
Magnesium sulfate		
Sodium carbonate		
Sodium bicarbonate		
Calcium chloride		
Sugar		

3. Table 2: After you mix the following substances, fill in the table with what happens when they interact, and with what properties you can observe in the products.

Reactants	Outcome of Interaction	Observable Properties of Product	Precipitate Density	Precipitate Solubility in Water
Magnesium sulfate + Sodium carbonate				
Sodium bicarbonate + Calcium chloride				
Sugar + water				

4. Are the properties of the reactants different than the properties of the products?

5. Is the precipitate or final product a different substance from either reactant?

6. How can you use the properties to determine if a chemical reaction has occurred?

1. What is scientific evidence?

2. How do scientists collect evidence that a chemical reaction has occurred?

3. What evidence suggests that burning sugar is a chemical reaction?

4. What are some properties that tend to be unique for each substance?

5. Why are these properties used to identify chemical reactions?

1. What is the relationship between salicin and salicylic acid?

2. What did early doctors think salicylic acid could treat?

3. What is a clinical trial?

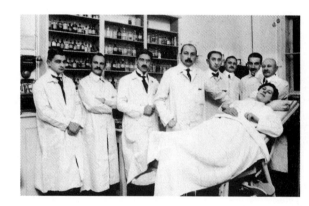

4. What is the relationship between salicylic acid and aspirin?

5. Why is aspirin a better medicine than salicylic acid?

MAKING SENSE OF PHENOMENA

Phenomenon: Mixing vinegar and baking soda causes the substances to bubble up and spill over a container's edge.

1. Use what you have learned to explain this phenomenon. Be sure to address these points in your explanation:

   • What properties differ between vinegar, baking soda, and carbon dioxide?

   • How do scientists know if a new substance has formed through a chemical reaction?

Identifying Chemical Reactions

Phenomenon: Burning steel wool causes the mass of the steel wool to increase.

1. What questions do you have about this phenomenon?

INVESTIGATION 1

Use the simulation to investigate chemical reactions. Then, throughout the investigation, fill out the prompts below. You will continue to build your conceptual model of chemical reactions and then will compare the simulation to the physical bodies model you create in class.

1. Summarize how your model describes a chemical reaction.

2. For each reaction, illustrate your model. Use circles of different colors to represent the different atoms and sticks to represent the bonds between the atoms.

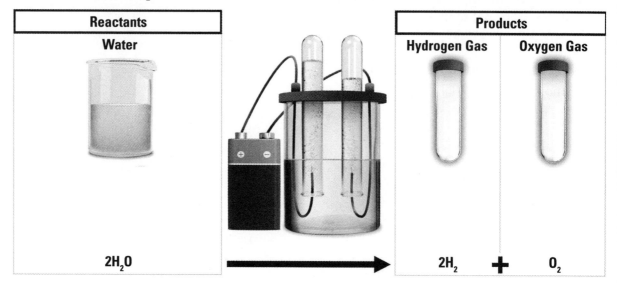

3. For each reaction, illustrate your model. Use circles of different colors to represent the different atoms and sticks to represent the bonds between the atoms.

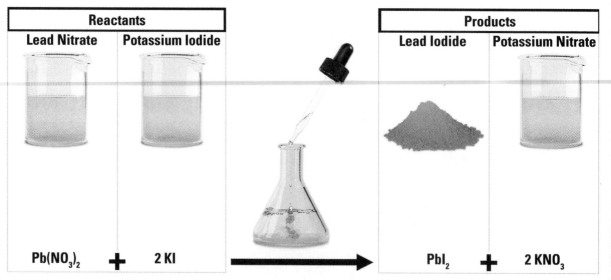

© Teachers' Curriculum Institute

4. For each reaction, illustrate your model. Use circles of different colors to represent the different atoms and sticks to represent the bonds between the atoms.

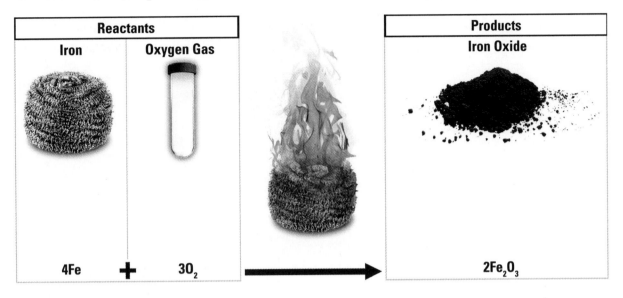

Reactants		Products
Iron	Oxygen Gas	Iron Oxide

$4Fe$ $+$ $3O_2$ $\longrightarrow$ $2Fe_2O_3$

5. For each reaction, illustrate your model. Use circles of different colors to represent the different atoms and sticks to represent the bonds between the atoms.

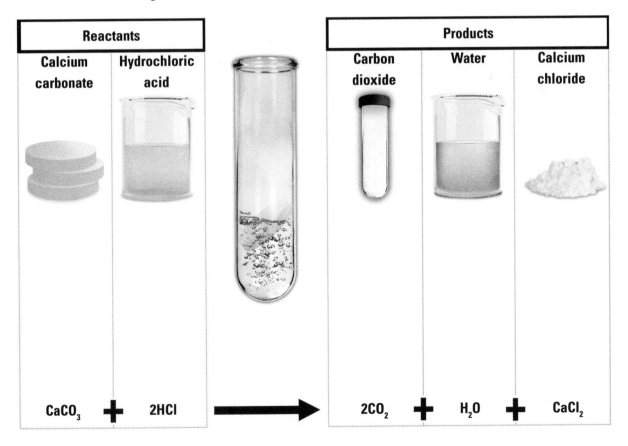

Reactants		Products		
Calcium carbonate	Hydrochloric acid	Carbon dioxide	Water	Calcium chloride

$CaCO_3$ $+$ $2HCl$ $\longrightarrow$ $2CO_2$ $+$ H_2O $+$ $CaCl_2$

6. For each reaction, illustrate your model. Use circles of different colors to represent the different atoms and sticks to represent the bonds between the atoms.

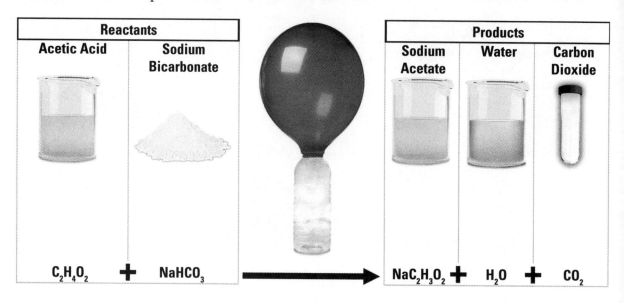

Reactants			Products	
Acetic Acid	Sodium Bicarbonate	Sodium Acetate	Water	Carbon Dioxide
$C_2H_4O_2$	$NaHCO_3$	$NaC_2H_3O_2$	H_2O	CO_2

7. In the Venn diagram, describe the similarities and differences between the two models you used to investigate atoms in chemical reactions.

Model 1: _____   **Model 2:** _____

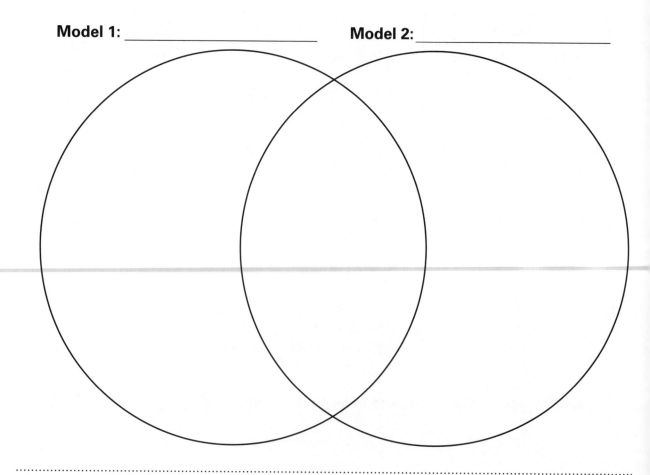

1. Annotate the image with the following labels:

    - Reactants
    - Products
    - Chemical bond

    Then, in red, circle the chemical bonds that break. In blue, circle the chemical bonds that formed.

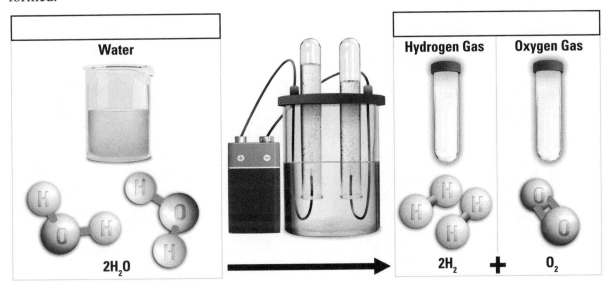

2. Annotate the image with the following labels:

    - Reactants
    - Products
    - Chemical bond

    Then, in red, circle the chemical bonds that break. In blue, circle the chemical bonds that formed.

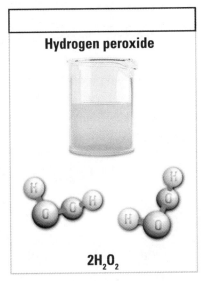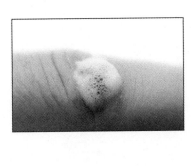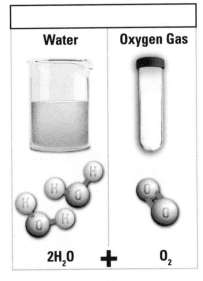

1. Annotate the image with the following labels:
   - Reactants
   - Products
   - Chemical bond

   Then, in red, circle the chemical bonds that break. In blue, circle the chemical bonds that formed.

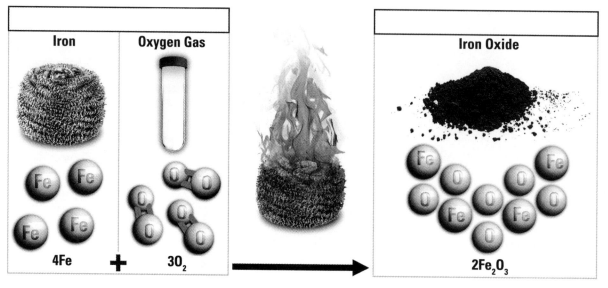

2. Annotate the image with the following labels:
   - Reactants
   - Products
   - Chemical bond

   Then, in red, circle the chemical bonds that break. In blue, circle the chemical bonds that formed.

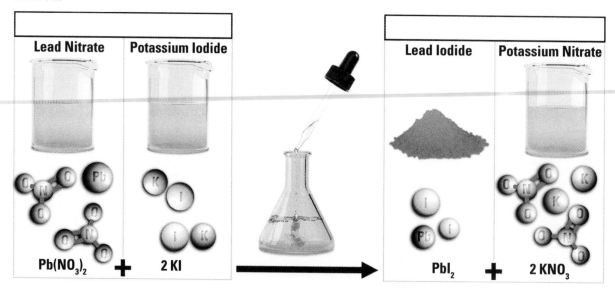

3. Summarize how atoms behave in chemical reactions. Be sure to use the phrases: *chemical bond*, *break apart*, *combine*, and *switch places*.

INVESTIGATION 2

1. According to your model, what changes during a chemical reaction? What stays the same?

2. Can you directly measure anything on the macroscopic scale to confirm that your model is accurate?

3. Record your data in the table below.

	Cup Mass (g)	Reactant 1 Mass (g)	Reactant 2 Mass (g)	Product Mass (g)	Change in Mass
Reaction A: magnesium sulfate + sodium carbonate					
Reaction B: sodium carbonate + calcium chloride					
Reaction C: acetic acid + sodium bicarbonate					

4. Explain how atoms behave in a chemical reaction.

5. Draw a model to accompany your explanation of how atoms behave in a chemical reaction.

Reactants	Products

Use the image to help fill in the table below.

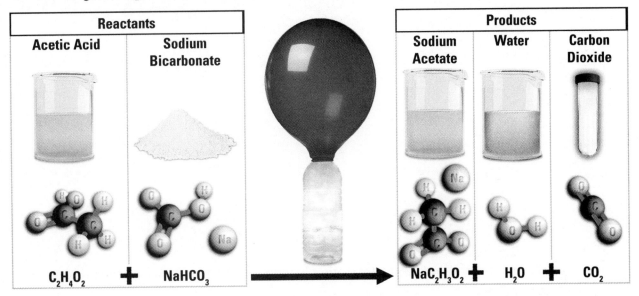

1. Fill out the following table with the number of each element in the chemical reaction.

	Reactants		Products		
	Acetic acid	Sodium bicarbonate	Sodium acetate	Water	Carbon dioxide
H					
C					
O					
Na					

2. Use the information in the table to explain why the mass does not change in a chemical reaction between acetic acid (vinegar) and sodium bicarbonate (baking soda).

1. Describe the green method of ibuprofen production and how this solved the problem of an inefficient process.

2. Describe the method of using products in other reactions and how this solved the problem of an inefficient process.

3. Describe how combining the two reactions helped solve the problem of an inefficient process.

MAKING SENSE OF PHENOMENA

Phenomenon: Burning steel wool causes the mass of the steel wool to increase.

1. Use what you have learned to explain this phenomenon. Be sure to address these points in your explanation:

   • What caused the mass to increase? Where did the mass come from?

   • If mass increased, how is matter conserved?

   • How can you model the chemical reaction of burning steel wool? What are the reactants and what are the products?

Energy in Chemical Reactions

OBSERVING PHENOMENA

Phenomenon: When magnesium is lit on fire it burns with a bright light. In contrast, when chicken is lit on fire, it changes color from pink to white.

1. What questions do you have about this phenomenon?

INVESTIGATION 1

1. Indicate if the chemical reaction is endothermic or exothermic by adding energy to the correct side of the equation. Then, model the chemical reaction by annotating the photo.

$$C_6H_{10}O_5 + 6O_2 \longrightarrow 6CO_2 + 5H_2O$$

2. Indicate if the chemical reaction is endothermic or exothermic by adding energy to the correct side of the equation. Then, model the chemical reaction by annotating the photo.

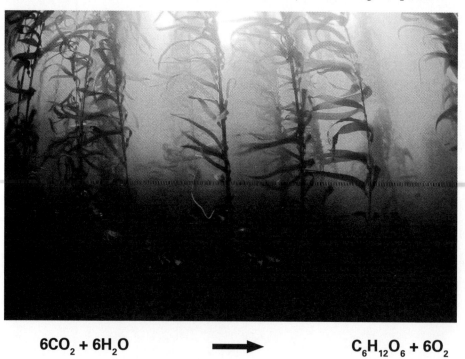

$$6CO_2 + 6H_2O \longrightarrow C_6H_{12}O_6 + 6O_2$$

3. Indicate if the chemical reaction is endothermic or exothermic by adding energy to the correct side of the equation. Then, model the chemical reaction by annotating the photo.

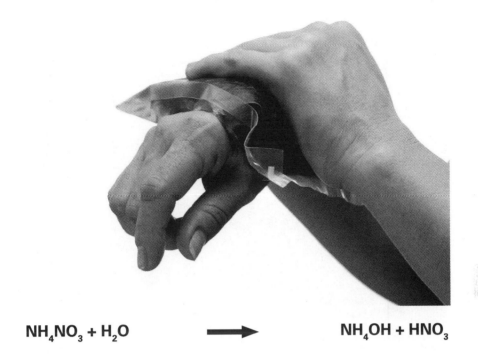

$$NH_4NO_3 + H_2O \longrightarrow NH_4OH + HNO_3$$

4. Indicate if the chemical reaction is endothermic or exothermic by adding energy to the correct side of the equation. Then, model the chemical reaction by annotating the photo.

$$2KClO_3 \longrightarrow 2KCl + 3O_2$$

1 - Exothermic Reactions

1. Model the flow of energy in the exothermic reaction shown below.

2 - Endothermic Reactions

1. Model the flow of energy in the endothermic reaction shown below.

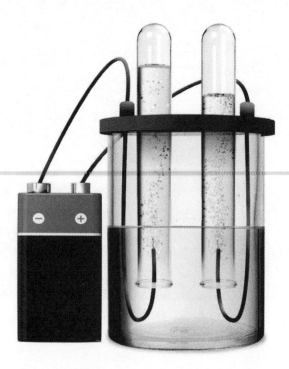

INVESTIGATION 2

Follow the directions to measure the change in temperature during chemical reactions.

a. Fill a cup with 100 mL of water.

b. Measure the temperature of the water using your thermometer.

c. Mix 1 tablespoon of your first reactant with 1 tablespoon of your second reactant.

d. Leave your thermometer in the chemical reaction. Record the highest or lowest temperature that the chemical reaction reaches.

e. Subtract the final temperature from the starting temperature.

1. Record your data here.

Reactant A	Reactant B	Starting Temperature (°C)	Final Temperature (°C)	Temperature Change (°C)
sodium bicarbonate (baking soda)	acetic acid (vinegar)			
magnesium sulfate (Epsom salt)	sodium carbonate			
sodium bicarbonate (baking soda)	calcium chloride			
ammonium chloride	water			
calcium chloride	water			

2. Indicate if the chemical reaction is endothermic or exothermic by adding energy to the correct side of the equation. Then, model the chemical reaction by annotating the photo.

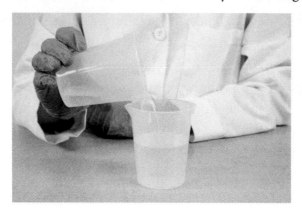

$$CH_3COOH + NaHCO_3 \longrightarrow CH_3COONa + CO_2 + H_2O$$

3. Indicate if the chemical reaction is endothermic or exothermic by adding energy to the correct side of the equation. Then, model the chemical reaction by annotating the photo.

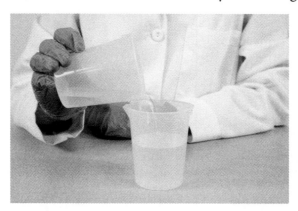

$$MgSO_4 + Na_2CO_3 \longrightarrow MgCO_3 + Na_2SO_4$$

4. Indicate if the chemical reaction is endothermic or exothermic by adding energy to the correct side of the equation. Then, model the chemical reaction by annotating the photo.

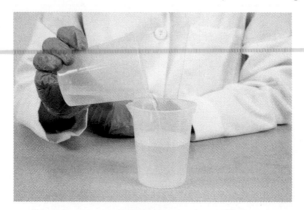

$$CaCl_2 + Na_2CO_3 \longrightarrow CaCO_3 + 2NaCl + H_2O + CO_2$$

5. Indicate if the chemical reaction is endothermic or exothermic by adding energy to the correct side of the equation. Then, model the chemical reaction by annotating the photo.

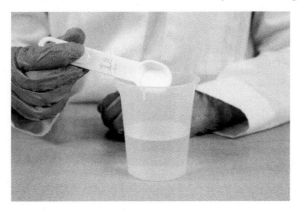

$NH_4Cl + H_2O$ $HCl + NH_4OH$

6. Indicate if the chemical reaction is endothermic or exothermic by adding energy to the correct side of the equation. Then, model the chemical reaction by annotating the photo.

$CaCl_2 + 2H_2O$ $Ca(OH)_2 + 2HCl$

7. Record your results in the table below. Be sure to indicate which how much reactant you actually used in each trial.

Trial	Planned Amount of Reactant (g)	Actual Amount of Reactant (g)	Starting Temperature (°C)	Final Temperature (°C)	Temperature Change (°C)

8. Summarize the conclusions your data shows. What is the cause and effect relationship between the amount of reactant you used and the temperature increase?

Plan your investigation to see how cold you can go.

9. Determine your variables.

My independent variable is	
I will adjust my independent variable by	
I will measure my independent variable by	
My dependent variable is	
I will measure my dependent variable by	
The variables I will control are	
I will keep them constant by	

10. Record the tools you will use.

Tools	Purpose of the Tool

11. Record the measurements you will take and where you will record them.

Measurement	Units	Recording Location

12. Record the steps you will take.

I will conduct _____ trials. In each trial, I will do the following steps.

1	
2	
3	
4	
5	
6	
7	
8	
9	
10	

1. Recall whether each chemical reaction is exothermic or endothermic. Then, add "energy" to the correct side of the chemical equation.

$$2C_4H_{10} + 13O_2 \longrightarrow 8CO_2 + 10H_2O$$

$$2H_2O \longrightarrow O_2 + 2H_2$$

Look at the graph of the temperature of the chemical reaction over time. Then, answer the following questions.

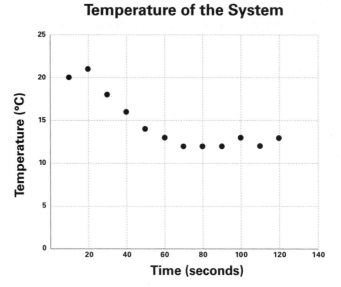

Temperature of the System

2. Is this chemical reaction exothermic or endothermic?

3. Annotate the illustration to describe the flow of energy between the chemical reaction and its environment. Then, edit the chemical equation to include the role of energy.

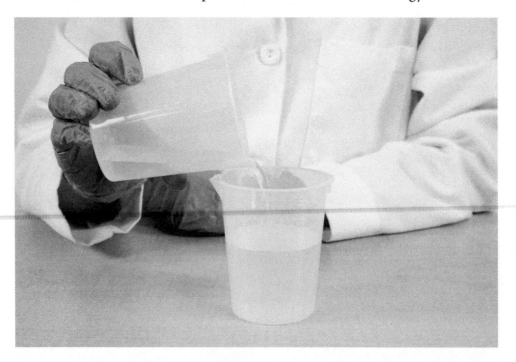

Reactant A + Reactant B ➡ Product A + Product B + Product C

1. Explain why a group of engineers would want to make a prototype.

2. Engineers test and modify their prototype multiple times. Explain the benefits of doing so.

3. Suppose you were designing a hand warmer for a ski trip. What steps would you take in the design process?

MAKING SENSE OF PHENOMENA

Phenomenon: When magnesium is lit on fire it burns with a bright light. In contrast, when chicken is lit on fire, it changes color from pink to white.

1. Use what you have learned to explain this phenomenon. Be sure to address these points in your explanation:

    •   How can you model the energy flow in these chemical reactions? Does energy flow in the same way in both of these situations?

    •   Can you track the energy throughout these chemical reactions?

Designing a Hot Pack

Defining the Engineering Problem

1. Your company has assigned you to design a one-time use hot pack. With your team, decide on the specific problem that you want to solve with a hot pack.

    HINTS:

    Do you want to treat an injury, such as back pain or a neck ache?

    Do you want to keep hands or feet warm in the winter?

2. Brainstorm possible criteria for success. Then brainstorm potential constraints.

    HINT:

    Freely brainstorm all the criteria and constraints you can think of. You'll narrow down this list later.

Criteria	Constraints

3. Your company has listed some non-negotiables below. From your initial list of criteria and constraints, decide as a team which additional criteria and constraints are the most important.

HINTS:

For the criteria, did you consider requirements needed to solve your specific problem? Portability? Size or shape?

For constraints, did you consider the amount and cost of materials? Safety issues?

When possible, assign a number value to your criteria and constraints.

Criteria for Success	Constraints for Solution
Device must function at 40°C for at least 5 minutes.	During all trials of the testing phase, limited to using no more than 200 g of calcium chloride total.
Device should use as little calcium chloride as possible.	

Developing Possible Solutions

1. Brainstorm two different solutions on your own. Sketch and label them below.

   HINT:

   Think outside the box! Try to come up with two totally different types of devices that use different types of materials.

My Design A

My Design B

Share your designs with your team, evaluating how well each design would meet the criteria and constraints.

2. Then, as a team, come up with a design for your first team prototype.

- Make a detailed drawing below.
- Label all the components of the system.
- Annotate how energy will be transferred and how you will track energy transfer.

HINTS:

If you are able to bring in additional materials, you may include those in your design.

Use what you learned in Lesson 8: Energy in Chemical Reactions, and your prior knowledge about hot packs, as you design your prototype.

First Team Prototype Design

Optimizing the Solution

1. Plan how you will build and test your first design by filling out the information below. (Important: Before carrying out your plan, you must get your materials and procedure approved for safety.)

HINTS:

Did you include safety equipment in your plan?

How will you track energy transfers in the system?

List the materials you will use. Give specific quantities for each.	
Explain the steps you will take to *build* your hot pack.	
Explain the steps you will take to *test* your hot pack.	
Explain the safety precautions you will take.	

2. Get teacher approval to build and test: _____

3. Test your device. Record quantitative and qualitative data below.

Calcium chloride (g)	Water (mL)	Starting temp (°C)	Highest temp (°C)	Time device stays above 40°C	Observations about how the device functions

4. Reflect on your first test.

    What aspects of your design met your criteria?

    What aspects of your design did not work well?

5. Brainstorm how you could improve your device.

   Sketch and label the key changes. For each change, annotate how you think it will help your device better meet the criteria and constraints.

6. Test your modified device and record results below. Continue modifying and retesting your device as long as time and materials allow.

Iteration #	Calcium chloride (g)	Water (mL)	Starting temp (°C)	Highest temp (°C)	Time device stays above 40°C	Observations about how the device functions

Engineering Challenge Assessment

Use the rubric below to evaluate your work on this engineering task. Then record your score in the Score column.

Engineering Process	Achievement Levels			Score
	Proficient (2 points)	**Emergent (1 point)**	**Not Present (0 points)**	
Defining the Engineering Problem	Identified design criteria (including the problem to be solved through the release of thermal energy via a device) and constraints on the solution with precision and clarity.	Understood the engineering task but the design criteria and constraints are not clearly identified.	Did not identify the design criteria and constraints of the engineering problem.	
Developing Possible Solutions	Identified components of the system in the design, including how thermal energy would be released and tracked.	Identified some components of the system in the design, but labeling may be incomplete or missing how energy is tracked.	Identified few to no components of the system in the design.	
	Evaluated competing individual and team design solutions based on agreed-upon criteria and constraints.	Evaluated competing design solutions, but did not base selections on design criteria.	Did not evaluate design solutions.	
Optimizing the Design Solution	Testing was done in a logical, systematic manner and produced results showing how well the device solved the problem.	Testing was done randomly or incompletely and produced incomplete results.	Conducted one or no tests.	
	Modified the design of the device based on testing, each time improving the design relative to the criteria and constraints.	Modified the device but in ways unrelated to testing results or to the criteria and constraints.	Did not modify the design of the device.	

Chemical Engineering and Society

Phenomenon: Faux leather is made from synthetic materials but can serve the same functions as real leather.

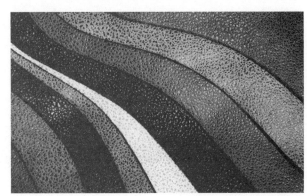

1. What questions do you have about this phenomenon?

© Teachers' Curriculum Institute   Chemical Engineering and Society **133**

INVESTIGATION 1

1. When do you think an author might be biased to write about the negative impact of DDT?

2. When do you think an author might be biased to write about the positive impact of DDT?

Understand the Controversy

3. What are the properties of SLS that make it useful in the products that contain it?

4. What natural resources provide the materials that are used to make SLS?

5. Given what you know now, who do you think you can believe when some people say a product is unsafe, but the government still approves its use? How would you figure out which information is accurate?

Compare Articles About SLS

6. Which Handout did you read?

7. Write out your opinion of how SLS impacts society in this space.

8. After discussing, has your opinion changed?

9. After reading all the Handouts, has your opinion changed?

10. How did scientists test whether SLS was harmful or not? What did they find?

11. What was the purpose of the story written for a magazine?

12. What was the purpose of the story written on a blog?

Learn About Different Kinds of Sources

13. What are some scientific organizations that you think would publish accurate scientific information?

14. When do you think it would make sense to use a blog as a source?

15. When would it make sense to use a newspaper or magazine as a source?

Apply Your Understanding of Sources

16. Fill in the table with what makes each source a good one or a bad one for each of the purposes listed.

Purpose	Handout A	Handout B	Handout C
Determining the safety of this chemical			
Understanding the history of public response to the chemical			
Brainstorming ideas about how to make healthy decisions in your life in general while being entertained			

17. Based on what you've learned, assess how well you think the claims in each handout are supported by evidence. Write: Very well supported, well supported, somewhat supported, or not supported.

Purpose	Handout A	Handout B	Handout C
How well are the claims in the handout supported by evidence?			

1. What is a synthetic material?

2. What materials are used to produce synthetic substances?

3. What makes synthetic materials useful to people?

4. What are three synthetic products made from the natural resource petroleum?

5. What's an example of a synthetic material that is produced even though it is also found in nature sometimes? Why would scientists make something that is also found in nature?

INVESTIGATION 2

Generate a List of Possible Topics

1. Write out a list of possible synthetic products to research here.

Choose a Topic

2. Choose which product or chemical you will focus on and write it down here.

Research Your Product

3. List five sources you will use in your advertisement.

Create an Advertisement

4. Write a script for your TV or radio advertisement here. Be sure to answer the following questions:

   - What are the properties of a synthetic chemical involved in the product?

   - What is the synthetic chemical made from? How is it made?

   - How does the synthetic chemical function in the product?

   Include five sources at the point of use. That means when you use information from the source, cite it either verbally or by showing a visual card of the information.

Perform Your Advertisement

5. Take notes on the sources used by each group here. Write down if a source is scientific or not and whether it seems accurate or biased.

Source 5								
Source 4								
Source 3								
Source 2								
Source 1								
Product Advertised								

6. As you watch the student advertisements and evaluate their sources, what kinds of bias do you recognize? Do you think advertisements in general are biased?

7. Did each group use all reliable resources? Was there any disagreement about this?

8. How do you think real advertisements might be biased in their use of data?

9. What other sources of information might show bias in their use of data?

1. Where does gasoline come from?

2. Can we make fuel from something other than fossil fuels? Explain. Why would we want to do that?

3. What material is made from glucose in corn?

4. List one benefit of ethanol as a fuel and one benefit of gasoline as a fuel.

1. What is a food additive?

2. Why would people prefer an artificial sweetener over natural sugar?

3. What makes sucralose different so that the body can't digest it?

4. Label which of the images is sucrose and which is sucralose. Then circle the three extra atoms that make sucralose hard for the body to digest.

5. Why might a person with diabetes choose to eat sucralose?

1. What is an example of a medicine that is produced by modifying a natural resource?

2. What is paclitaxel? Where does it come from? What does it treat?

3. Why can't we just forever harvest Pacific Yew trees to get the materials needed to make this drug?

4. How did scientists solve the problem of making enough paclitaxel?

1. What are the properties of plastic that make it so useful to people?

2. What are some problems caused by plastic's properties?

3. What is a solution to this problem that engineers are developing?

4. What are some organisms that help break down materials that are biodegradable?

5. What is the problem with PLA?

6. How can we help the environment while we wait for engineers to develop a great biodegradable plastic?

MAKING SENSE OF PHENOMENA

Phenomenon: Faux leather is made from synthetic materials but can serve the same functions as real leather.

1. Use what you have learned to explain this phenomenon. Be sure to address these points in your explanation:

    •   Where does faux leather come from?

    •   How does society use faux leather?

Modifying and Explaining Survival Gear

The new reality show "The Next Top Survivalist" is looking for applicants! They are looking for people who can explain how hot packs and butane torches release heat when they are activated.

You will get in groups of four and tell them why you and your group are qualified to be a contestant through a video audition. Impress the producers of the show with your knowledge of chemistry.

Performance Assessment Requirements

Your video audition for "The Next Top Survivalist" should include:

- a design for a hot pack that helps battle hypothermia.
- ideas for how to improve the hot pack design.
- a report on the origins of calcium chloride.
- an analysis of the properties of substances involved before and after butane is burned.
- a 3D model of what happens to butane when it burns.
- a script that explains the burning butane reaction.

_____ Step 1: Modifying a Hypothermia Pack

Show the producers of "The Next Top Survivalist" how you can modify a hypothermia pack design to meet the following criteria:

- reach 50 degrees Celsius.
- stay warm for as long as possible.

Examine one design for the pack in _Handout: Hypothermia Pack_. Was the design able to meet the criteria?

Write out the chemical equation for this reaction. Put the reactants and products in the correct place.

- $CaCl_2$ (calcium chloride)
- $Ca(OH)_2$ (calcium hydroxide)
- (+ energy)

- $2HCl$ (hydrochloric acid)
- $2H_2O$ (water)

Which of the reactants in this reaction will increase the temperature? How can you modify the hypothermia pack design to better meet the criteria?

Come up with a design for the hypothermia pack to better meet the criteria.

_____ **Step 2: Testing and Improving the Hypothermia Pack Design**

Test your hypothermia pack design. Record your results below.

Trial	Amount of CaCl$_2$ used	Maximum temperature	Length of time
1			
2			
3			
4			
5			

Write a script for your video audition that tells the process you went through to modify the hypothermia pack. Show the producers how much you know about battling hypothermia by describing:

- the chemical reaction involved in the hypothermia pack. Make sure to describe how energy flows in this reaction.
- how you improved the design for the hypothermia pack and how the materials and shape of it make it good for releasing heat.
- your results from testing your design and ideas for how you can improve it.

_____ Step 3: Researching the History of Calcium Chloride

Show the producers your knowledge of calcium chloride. Research answers to these questions:

- Where does calcium chloride come from? How can it be synthesized?
- Can calcium chloride be mass produced?
- What are calcium chloride's physical and chemical properties?
- How is calcium chloride useful for people?

Find sources that that help answer these questions. Then determine if the source is credible.

Information About Calcium Chloride	Source	Is this source credible? What are the potential biases?

Write a script for your video audition that uses the information you researched. Show the producers how much you know about how calcium chloride is used in survival gear by answering these questions in your script:

- Where does calcium chloride come from? How can it be synthesized?
- Can calcium chloride be mass produced?
- What are calcium chloride's physical and chemical properties?
- How is calcium chloride useful for people

_____ **Step 4: Understanding What Happens When Butane Burns**

The data in this chart shows how the properties of butane changed before and after it is burned.

	Butane gas C_4H_{10}	Oxygen gas O_2	Carbon Dioxide gas CO_2	Water Vapor H_2O
Reactant/Product	Reactant	Reactant	Product	Product
Density compared to Air	2.11	1.1	1.67	0.804
Boiling Point	-0.5	-183.1	-78.5	100
Flammability	Yes	No	No	No
Solubility	No information	No information	No information	No information
Odor	No	No	No	No

What are the properties of butane before it burned? After it burned?

What evidence tells you if a chemical reaction took place? Support your answer using data from the chart.

Complete the chemical equation for burning butane. Put the reactants and products in the correct place.

- 2 C_4H_{10} (butane gas)
- 8 CO_2 (carbon dioxide)
- (+ energy)

- 10 H_2O (water vapor)
- 13 O_2 (oxygen)

_____ Step 5: Making a Model of Burning Butane

Examine the atomic structure of each molecule, and identify them.

- Label each molecule as: butane, carbon dioxide, oxygen, or water vapor.
- State if it is the reactant or product in the reaction.

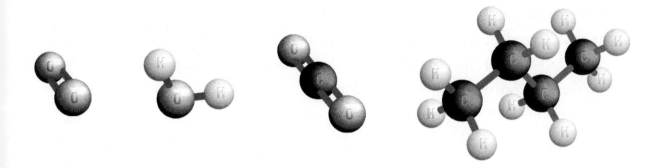

Show what happens when butane burns on an atomic level. Plan a model of burning butane by drawing a diagram of what happens before and after the reactants interact. Draw and label the molecules and their parts. Make sure you include energy in your model.

Create a 3D model of the molecules involved in burning butane based on your diagram. You can use clay, paper, or other supplies. You should be able to use this model in your video application to visually show what happens to butane molecules when they interact with oxygen and burn. Make sure your audience knows what each part of your model represents.

Write a script for your video audition to accompany the model of burning butane. Your script should describe:

- what happens during a burning butane reaction.
- the reactants and the type and number of molecules that make up the reactants.
- the products and the type and number of molecules that make up the products.
- how the atoms rearrange during the reaction.
- whether or not matter is conserved in this reaction.

_____ **Step 6: Filming Your Video Audition**

Put your video audition together! Use your scripts and models as you film your audition.

Performance Assessment Rubric

Use the rubric to evaluate your work on this Performance Assessment.

Dimension	Achievement Levels			Score
	Proficient (2 points)	**Emergent (1 point)**	**Not Present (0 points)**	
Science and Engineering Practices Analyzing and Interpreting Data *Analyze and interpret data to determine similarities and differences in findings.*	Analyzed and interpreted data about properties of butane before and after it is burned.	Analyzed and interpreted data about properties of butane before and after it is burned, but interpretations had some inaccuracies.	Did not analyze or interpret data about properties of butane before and after it is burned.	
Developing and Using Models *Develop a model to describe unobservable mechanisms.*	Developed a model to describe the atomic-level behavior of butane when it is burned.	Developed a model to describe the atomic-level behavior of butane when it is burned, but the model had some inaccuracies.	Did not develop a model to describe the atomic-level behavior of butane when it is burned, or the model had many inaccuracies.	
Explanations and Designing Solutions *Undertake a design project, engaging in the design cycle, to construct and/or implement a solution that meets specific design criteria and constraints.*	Used the engineering design cycle to modify a hot pack to reach specific design criteria and constraints.	Used the engineering design cycle to modify a hot pack, but design did not reach specific design criteria and constraints.	Did not use the engineering design cycle to modify a hot pack to reach specific design criteria and constraints.	
Obtaining, Evaluating, and Communicating Information *Gather, read, and synthesize information from multiple appropriate sources and assess the credibility, accuracy, and possible bias of each publication and methods used, and describe how they are supported or not supported by evidence.*	Researched the origins of calcium chloride and explained whether it was mass-producible given the sources used.	Researched the origins of calcium chloride and explained whether it was mass-producible, but may not have cited all sources.	Did not research the origins of calcium chloride nor explain whether it was mass-producible given the sources used.	

| Dimension | Achievement Levels | | | Score |
	Proficient (2 points)	Emergent (1 point)	Not Present (0 points)	
Crosscutting Concepts Patterns *Macroscopic patterns are related to the nature of microscopic and atomic-level structure.*	Used macroscopic patterns as evidence for whether or not a chemical reaction has occurred when burning butane.	Used macroscopic patterns to identify whether or not a chemical reaction has occurred when burning butane, but did not fully use the patterns as evidence.	Did not use macroscopic patterns to identify whether or not a chemical reaction has occurred when burning butane.	
Energy and Matter *Matter is conserved because atoms are conserved in physical and chemical processes.* *The transfer of energy can be tracked as energy flows through a designed or natural system.*	Used a model of burning butane to show that matter is conserved.	Used a model of burning butane to show that matter is conserved, but model may have some inaccuracies.	Did not make a model of burning butane, or model does not show matter is conserved.	
Structure and Function *Structures can be designed to serve particular functions by taking into account properties of different materials, and how materials can be shaped and used.*	Used chemical equations to show how energy flows in a chemical reaction of mixing calcium chloride and water and burning butane.	Used chemical equations to show how energy flows in a chemical reaction of mixing calcium chloride and water and burning butane, but chemical equations may have some inaccuracies.	Did not use chemical equations to show how energy flows in a chemical reaction of mixing calcium chloride and water and burning butane.	
	Explained how the materials used in the hot pack and the shape and design of the hot pack made it good for releasing heat.	Described the materials used in the hot pack and the shape and design of it, but did not full connect how the structure makes the hot pack good for releasing heat.	Did not explain how the materials used in the hot pack and the shape and design of the hot pack made it good for releasing heat.	

Dimension	Achievement Levels			Score
	Proficient (2 points)	Emergent (1 point)	Not Present (0 points)	
Disciplinary Core Ideas PS1.A: Structure and Properties of Matter *Each pure substance has characteristic physical and chemical properties (for any bulk quantity under given conditions) that can be used to identify it.*	Discussed both the macroscopic properties and the atomic behavior of different chemical reaction of burning butane in the video script.	Discussed either the macroscopic properties or the atomic behavior of different chemical reaction of burning butane in the video script.	Did not discuss the macroscopic properties nor the atomic behavior of different chemical reaction of burning butane in the video script.	
PS1.B: Chemical Reactions *Substances react chemically in characteristic ways. In a chemical process, the atoms that make up the original substances are regrouped into different molecules, and these new substances have different properties from those of the reactants.* *The total number of each type of atom is conserved, and thus the mass does not change.* *Some chemical reactions release energy, others store energy.*	Used chemical equations and models to show that mass is conserved because atoms are conserved when butane is burned.	Used chemical equations and models to show that mass is conserved because atoms are conserved when butane is burned, but the equations or models may have some inaccuracies.	Did not use chemical equations nor models to show that mass is conserved because atoms are conserved when butane is burned.	
ETS1.B: Developing Possible Solutions *A solution needs to be tested, and then modified on the basis of the test results, in order to improve it. (secondary to MS-PS1-6)*	Used chemical equations and models to show that energy can be released in a chemical reaction where butane is burned.	Used chemical equations and models to show that energy can be released in a chemical reaction where butane is burned, but the equations or models may have some inaccuracies.	Did not use chemical equations nor models to show that energy can be released in a chemical reaction where butane is burned.	
ETS1.C: Optimizing the Design Solution *Although one design may not perform the best across all tests, identifying the characteristics of the design that performed the best in each test can provide useful information for the redesign process - that is, some of the characteristics may be incorporated into the new design. (secondary to MS-PS1-6)*	Modified and tested a hot pack to improve its capacity for releasing energy and reaching a higher temperature.	Modified a hot pack to improve its capacity for releasing energy and reaching a higher temperature, but may not have tested the solution.	Did not a hot pack to improve its capacity for releasing energy and reaching a higher temperature.	
The iterative process of testing the most promising solutions and modifying what is proposed on the basis of the test results leads to greater refinement and ultimately to an optimal solution. (secondary to MS-PS1-6)	Identified the component that led to the greatest increase in temperature (amount of $CaCl_2$) and made adjustments accordingly in the redesign.	Identified the component that led to the greatest increase in temperature (amount of $CaCl_2$) and made adjustments accordingly in the redesign, but adjustments may not have better met the criteria and constraints.	Did not identify the component that led to the greatest increase in temperature (amount of $CaCl_2$) nor made adjustments accordingly in the redesign.	

Cover and Title Page:
Getty Images

Front Matter
vT: Tetra Images/Alamy vC: Perennou
Nuridsany/Science Source vB: GIPhotoStock/
Science Source

Unit 1, Unit Overview
2: Pond5

Unit 1, Lesson 1
3T: Thinkstock 3BL: Thinkstock 3BR: Thinkstock
10T: Wikipedia 10B: Wikimedia

Unit 1, Lesson 2
15L: Shutterstock 15LC: iStockphoto
15RC: iStockphoto 15R: iStockphoto

Unit 1, Lesson 3
27T: Thinkstock 29: Thinkstock 35T: Thinkstock
35B: Thinkstock 38: Martyn F. Chillmaid/Science
Source

Unit 2, Unit Overview
48: Pond5

Unit 2, Lesson 4
49: Charles D. Winters/Science Source

Unit 2, Lesson 5
61T: Jerry Whaley/Alamy 61B: Shutterstock
64: Thinkstock

Unit 3, Unit Overview
82: Pond5

Unit 3, Lesson 6
83T: David Taylor/Science Source 83B: Pond5
88: Dorling Kindersley/UIG/Science Source
89: Jan Sučko/Dreamstime 93: Thinkstock
94: Jonathan Kirn/Getty Images

Unit 3, Lesson 7
97: Thinkstock

Unit 3, Lesson 8
109T: Thinkstock 109BL: Pond5 109BR: Pond5
110T: Pond5 110B: Pond5 111T: Pond5
111B: Pond5 112T: Thinkstock

Unit 3, Lesson 9
133T: Pascal Goetgheluck/Science Source
133BL: Shutterstock 133BR: Shutterstock
138: Scott Bauer/US Department of Agriculture/
Science Source 143: Jim West/Alamy 145: Greg
Vaughn/Alamy 146: Image Source Salsa/Alamy